5

7800

listening
skills

IAN MACKAY

Second edition

Management Shapers is a comprehensive series covering all the crucial management skill areas. Each book includes the key issues, helpful starting points and practical advice in a concise and lively style. Together, they form an accessible library reflecting current best practice – ideal for study or quick reference.

The Chartered Institute of Personnel and Development is the leading publisher of books and reports for personnel and training professionals, students, and all those concerned with the effective management and development of people at work. For full details of all our titles, please contact the Publishing Department:

tel. 020-8263 3387

fax 020-8263 3850

e-mail publish@cipd.co.uk

The catalogue of all CIPD titles can be viewed on the CIPD website:

www.cipd.co.uk/publications

listening
skills

IAN MACKAY

Second edition
revised and updated by
Krystyna Weinstein

CHARTERED INSTITUTE OF PERSONNEL AND DEVELOPMENT

First published 1984 by the British Association for Commercial and Industrial Education, entitled *A Guide to Listening*.
Second edition 1995
First published in the *Training Extras* series in 1995
Reprinted 1997
First published in the *Management Shapers* series in 1998
Reprinted 2000

Typesetting by Paperweight
Printed in Great Britain by
The Guernsey Press, Channel Islands

British Library Cataloguing in Publication Data
A catalogue record for this book is available from the British Library

ISBN
0-85292-754-1

Chartered Institute of Personnel and Development, CIPD House, Camp Road, London SW19 4UX
Tel.: 020 8971 9000   Fax: 020 8263 3333
E-mail: cipd@cipd.co.uk   Website: www.cipd.co.uk
Incorporated by Royal Charter. Registered charity no. 1079797

contents

Other titles in the series:

introduction

Even before you were born you started to develop a vital skill, one which you have used continuously ever since. It is probably the most significant skill at your disposal. It has had a marked effect on your development in the past, and it will continue to do so in the future. And yet it is virtually certain that you have had no help in developing this skill. You have learned the other basic communication skills – speaking, reading and writing. But have you ever really learned to listen?

Consider for a moment the importance of effective listening in your life: conversations with friends and family, business meetings, discussion, conferences, interviews, talks, lectures – the list is endless and the ability to listen is central to all of them. Now ask yourself how your family, your colleagues or your close friends would rate your listening skill. More important – how do *you* rate it?

Whatever your answer, the following pages may help you to develop this skill further.

1 why is listening important?

Listening is the key to success. It enables you to do more than just hear what others are saying. Real listening means giving them your full attention, and understanding them. By listening you develop a deeper appreciation of what your colleagues at work are doing, how they are feeling, and why; at home you understand more fully your family's hopes, fears, and problems.

Listening opens up new horizons. It is the key to learning. In fact it is difficult to imagine how you could be successful without also being a good listener. In the pages that follow you will begin to understand what it is to be a really effective listener. And as you become increasingly successful at listening you will recognise changes in yourself. Other people will recognise it also, and at least part of the pleasure of succeeding is that it is recognised by others.

In recognising you as a good listener people will say that they can come to you to talk about issues that concern them; that you helped them resolve questions – simply by listening and allowing them to hear themselves speak; that you made them feel you understood (even if you didn't agree); that you didn't interrupt or impose yourself on them; and that you respect them and what they have to say.

But perhaps the greatest benefit of listening well to others is that they will reciprocate and listen to you, and respond when you are speaking. And the more you and they listen, the more you will all gain and learn.

Why do we listen?

We may have many reasons for listening to someone:

- to gain information
- to get feedback
- to participate in another's story
- to hear of their experiences and insights
- to be 'in control' (information is power)
- to broaden our horizons, ie to learn
- to create a relationship
- to respect and value others.

In other words, listening is more than just sitting passively and letting sound waft over you! But real listening, as we shall see, is not simply a case of paying attention to what is being said. It is also about being sensitive to the other person's:

- voice
- choice of words

▲ tone

◉ speed

◉ body, ie their body language.

Listening – something we do for so much of our time – is perhaps one of the most important skills we have, yet it is one that is least recognised. And it isn't recognised because people confuse it with hearing. But listening – as you will discover – involves much more than simply hearing.

A neglected skill

Looking back on your life, how many hours do you think you have spent listening to other people speak: at home, at school or college, or at work? As children we begin to learn through listening; in fact it's how we ourselves learn to speak. Later, at school or college, it's how we acquire knowledge – in lectures, seminars, and tutorial groups. At home it's how we know when children are happy or sad, or when a husband or wife is feeling tired or angry. At work it is the key to working well with others. Misheard instructions, half-grasped requests for information, progressively distorted messages passing along the line – all these result in unnecessary misunderstandings, lack of morale, and lower productivity. Clients and customers are dissatisfied, requests and orders are not met, a promised service is not provided.

Research reveals, however, that although we spend so much of our time 'listening' we don't necessarily remember all we're told. Shortly after a 10-minute oral presentation the average listener will have retained only half of what was said. After 48 hours they are likely to remember only 10 per cent!

As organisations – be they private companies or public institutions – increasingly recognise the importance of listening they are running communication courses where developing listening skills plays a large part. We are all realising that having specialised technical or professional skills, or a mass of information at our fingertips, is not sufficient if we are to achieve our working goals. We need to be able to share it with others and hear – by listening – what they need from us. But more importantly we need to value and take advantage of others around us: of their expertise, knowledge, ideas, and insights.

In short we need to respect others, and one of the key ways of showing that we respect them is to listen to them. By listening we also begin to 'empower' them, for they gain confidence in what they have to say, and they see it is useful and valued.

why don't we listen?

There are a number of reasons why we don't listen well. We'll look at each of them in turn.

Selective listening

As an introduction to this topic, try the following exercise with a partner:

Sit still for about five minutes with your eyes shut. Concentrate on the things you can hear, and identify as many different sounds as you can. At the end of the five minutes make a list, independently, of these sounds. Finally, discuss the results with your partner. What conclusions can be drawn about listening?

One of the conclusions may be that under normal circumstances we are selective in our listening. Sounds which are considered unimportant are shut out. We concentrate primarily on what we think is important.

To emphasise this point try reading the following passage, quite slowly, to different people. Tell them you will be asking just one question when you have finished. The results will probably surprise you.

Go to the left luggage locker (no. 252) at St Pancras station. In the locker you will find a cash box which contains the following:

$$52 \times \text{£1 notes}$$
$$10 \times \text{50p pieces}$$
$$\text{and}\quad 20 \times \text{10p coins}$$

Please bring me 25 £1 notes, two 50p pieces and all the 10p coins. What is the number of the locker?

Is it 522, 255, 252 or 525?

Many people will be overconcerned with the sums involved (the total amount of money in the cash box, the amount to be removed etc) because they have anticipated the question. The chances are that they will not remember the number of the locker and may even say, in justification, that you haven't told them! Why is this? Why do people listen, selectively, only to what they think is important? Part of the answer to this question lies in consideration of the next point.

Talking speed *v* speed of thought

There is a considerable difference between the speed at which people talk and the speed at which they think. The average person speaks at about 125 words per minute, whereas thinking speed is in the region of 500 words per minute. We all think a lot faster than we realise! The result is that when listening to someone we are continually jumping ahead of what is actually being said. And what do we think about whilst we are waiting for the speaker to catch up? The answer is of course anything and everything. We may be composing our response to what we've heard – but in the process be missing what is currently being said. Or we may be thinking of that stimulating conversation last night, the prospect of a pleasant weekend ahead, the local team's chances in the league – anything to help pass the time agreeably. In a word we tend to 'daydream'. As a result we 'tune out' much of what we hear. How often do you rejoin a conversation with a guilty start to realise that a response is expected and you have no idea what has just been said? And in another context – how often do you go for a mental 'walkabout' when you are listening to a talk or lecture?

Here is another exercise which may help to make the point. Again you will need a willing helper to whom the following passage can be read:

You are the leader of a search party looking for a plane which has crashed in the wilderness. After searching the area for some time you eventually locate deep furrows made by the plane as it crash-landed. Following the furrows you see the plane with its back broken lying partially submerged in the middle of a river. There is no obvious sign of life. You realise that there is no way you can carry the dead back to civilisation and you must choose where to bury them. It would be easier to get them to the far bank but the ground is very rocky. To bring them to the near bank would be much more difficult because of the depth of the water and speed of the current, but once on the bank the job would be relatively easy because the ground is soft.

On which side of the river would you bury the survivors?

Even if your listener has remained 'tuned in' whilst you were reading the chances are that although the last word, 'survivors', will be heard, its significance will not be acted upon. Why? Because if you have caught the listener's interest it will be in terms of the relative advantages of each river bank for the purpose at hand. Thoughts will be centred on a judicious weighing of the alternatives available – the precise impact of the final question will be an assumption. Certainly the words will be heard but will be peripheral to what is assumed to be the central issue – the choice of a burial ground. It isn't only airplanes which have an automatic pilot!

A phrase in the previous paragraph – 'catching the listener's interest' – introduces another reason which explains why we tend to be poor listeners, at least in some circumstances.

Lack of interest

How often do you really listen to a subject when you are not interested in it? When it bores you? As listeners we have a tendency to rate a speaker's subject on a continuum somewhere between 'very interesting' at one extreme to 'a crashing bore' at the other. If for instance you have a positive aversion to things mechanical consider your reaction to some mechanical genius who relates to you how he stripped his car engine down at the roadside, carried out the necessary repairs, put everything back together again, and drove off. The talk would be of gaskets, pistons, valve seats, con rods, gaps of so many 'thou', and so on. Would you really listen?

Next time you are listening to someone talk on a subject you find uninteresting check how long it is before you switch off or move away (if you can!).

On the other hand you may think you're bored by a subject, but if you just stopped to listen you might in fact find it more compelling than you thought. And then there are occasions when you're not interested but have to listen, because what the other person is telling you directly affects your work. Such may be the case when the production supervisor tells you of the breakdown on one of his sections, when you are simply interested in meeting customer requests for spare parts. Understanding (ie listening to the supervisor's problem) becomes important, for without that understanding you won't be able to reach some way of tackling the issue of angry and dissatisfied customers.

Yet there are times when you genuinely have other things on your mind (a sick child, an urgent job, a train to catch) and you find listening to, and concentrating on, other issues almost impossible.

If any of these instances arise the person to whom we are meant to be listening will hopefully pick up our non-listening behaviour, which will be very marked: staring into the distance, sitting on the edge of our chair, moving towards the door, packing our bag, and saying 'yes' or 'no' with no conviction or energy in our voice. In these instances it is not only we who are listeners. The other person also becomes one.

Beliefs and attitudes

We all have opinions on a variety of current issues; we feel strongly about certain subjects; we value certain behaviours.

Consider your reaction if a speaker challenges your beliefs, attitudes, or opinions. Although she may be totally unaware that what she is saying represents a challenge, how do you feel? Do you start to get emotionally involved and return the challenge? Because this is a recipe for heated argument, it could never be called effective listening! Emotional involvement always makes it more difficult for you to assess what is being said. Unless you 'hear her out' you will never hear the full story. It does pay to reserve judgement and then respond with a reasoned reply, rather than adopt the 'Yes, but … ' approach. To understand 'with' the person who is talking to you rather than to evaluate and prejudge her message is one of the marks of the effective listener.

Admittedly if your cherished beliefs are criticised then you may well take it personally – you will probably feel threatened. There is no disputing the fact that listening can be positively dangerous – it can be harmful to your self-image and you do run the risk of being changed yourself. But the risk may be worthwhile. Consider for a moment the words of Elton Mayo, which seem particularly appropriate in this context: 'One friend, one person who is truly understanding, who takes the trouble to listen to us as we consider our problems, can change our whole outlook on the world'.

Reactions to the speaker

Another reason why we tend to listen less effectively than we might concerns our reaction to the speaker rather than the opinions he happens to be expressing. As Emerson once said – 'What you are sounds so loudly in my ears that I can't hear what you say.' To make this point, take a few moments to consider your answer to the following question.

What are the things (such as 'class', accent, style of dress, mannerisms etc) about people that are likely to provoke a strong reaction (annoyance, anger, embarrassment etc) in you?

These and other related factors do have an effect on the way we listen, but only you can judge for yourself which ones have such a negative effect on you. For example, one person's pet dislike may be expressed in the following words: 'I just can't stand people who talk in that upper-class drawl and who look down their noses at you!' Pity the poor inoffensive individual who just happens to be well over six feet tall and talks like that because it is the only way he knows how. Whatever he says will not be listened to. The 'listener' will be too busy criticising *him* rather than what he says.

In this case it is possibly the accent which is the main stumbling-block. For other people it may be the speaker's mannerisms which are the distraction. We have all come across people who wave their arms around, who keep pushing their glasses back up to the bridge of their nose, or who 'wash their hands' whilst speaking. Of the numerous possibilities, which particularly annoy you? Whatever your answer, if someone is talking to you *and* acting in a particular way which irritates or annoys you, will you really be listening to what is said?

This leads on to another obstacle which people can find distracting: the speaker's use of words.

Our preconceptions

Our preconceptions often mean we don't even give another person a chance to speak. We prejudge what they have to say from who they are, and dismiss them out of hand. We simply don't value what they might have to offer. People in organisations rarely, for instance, listen to cleaners and porters, gardeners and kitchen staff, filing clerks and others who carry out so-called 'menial' (in reality essential) tasks not considered crucial to the work of the organisation. We make assumptions about their ability to have anything of importance to tell us. This is so often wrong – as well as being insulting to them.

Others who are often marginalised in this way are so-called minorities: a racial minority, people with disabilities, or (in some offices) even women – even though they represent just over half the population!

The words we hear

As speakers ourselves, we all tend to have pet words and phrases which we trot out at the least opportunity. When combined with current catchwords and phrases they may present a powerful barrier to effective listening. (How do you react to these examples picked at random from those currently in use – 'at the end of the day' and 'at this moment in time'?) If these particular phrases don't bother you as a listener, which might?

Think back to your time at school. Was there a member of staff who was known for unswerving devotion to particular words and phrases? And did you place bets on the number of times such words and phrases were used in the space of a 40-minute class? And what is your reaction if you hear these same words and phrases today?

Over-repetition of words and phrases is one distraction. The use of unfamiliar words is another. Some speakers fall into the trap of using 'jargon' and other technical words and abbreviations which may be foreign to you as the listener. This can tend to happen particularly when someone is trying to impress you with his expertise. How do you feel? Do you spend more time getting irritated or do you ask yourself what it tells you about the speaker? There are nearly half a million words in the English language although the average person uses a tiny proportion – maybe 3–4,000 only. Using words that others don't understand may result in them (or you, if you're the listener!) 'switching off'.

Yet another distraction is the use of particular words which may provoke an emotional reaction in you as the listener. One example is words indicating racial discrimination, an issue about which you may well feel strongly. Another example is the use of profane language, which you might find utterly distasteful when you hear it. Even this last example might produce an over reaction: 'Why "profane language" rather than "swearing" – why not call a spade a spade rather than a long-handled digging implement?' Why indeed? It is worth remembering that we all harbour strong feelings about certain words (and the use of a number of words when just one would do) and these words do tend to get in the way of effective listening.

A final point: it is worth remembering that the same words mean different things to different people. What we hear or understand when someone speaks to us is largely shaped by our own experience and background. Take two short, everyday words: to 'help' someone, and to go for a 'walk'.

Even these can have various meanings. 'Help' can mean 'we'll do it for you', or 'we'll give you a hand', and anything in between; but we'll hear whatever it is we want to hear when the word is uttered (unless, of course, we check out what the speaker meant!). 'To go for a walk' could mean 'a stroll round the garden' or 'a day's hike'. The fact is that we generally understand the relevant meaning of a particular word by the context in which it is used But not always. Consider such abstract words, so widely used in organisations, as 'facilities', 'possibilities', or 'conditions' to name but three of a long list of abstract words whose meaning is only clear when explained and defined by the speaker. So, do 'facilities' mean the toilets, the telephones or the parking spaces?

In other words, what we often hear or understand when someone speaks to us is largely shaped by our own experiences, needs, or background. We hear what our minds tell us the other person has said. We have preconceived notions of what people mean when they speak. These preconceived ideas are examples of what psychologists call a mind-set – a readiness to perceive. Perhaps the problems associated with this readiness to perceive – sometimes correctly, often incorrectly – may be summed up by the following words, which appeared on a notice in the Pentagon:

I know you believe you understand what you think I said, but I am not sure you realise that what you heard is not what I meant.

Physical distractions

Another factor that interferes with effective listening can be summed up in two words – physical distraction. This can be a problem for many people and it comes in a number of different guises.

First there is the distraction of noise. It is very difficult to listen well if your ears are being assaulted by a variety of interfering sounds. Consider for a moment a situation in which you are trying to listen to a speaker and at the same time half-listening to another conversation elsewhere in the room. How effective will you be in achieving either aim?

And what about the noises you don't want to hear when you are trying to listen? The near-paralysing effect of some pop music at home, the insistent sound of a pneumatic drill in the road outside, the intermittent sounds of the traffic, the wailing of a police siren – all may distract you to a point where you will not be listening.

Sounds can distract you. So can sights: the interesting chart on the wall behind the speaker, the picture on the calendar which brings back happy memories, the confidential report you can't quite see from where you are standing, but which would make fascinating reading – the variety of potentially distracting sights is endless. But again these sights will only be distracting if you let them.

To allow ourselves to be distracted is yet another indication of poor listening. So what can you do to improve your own listening habits? Are there any particular guidelines for developing your personal skills as a listener? It is these questions which are considered next.

Another form of physical distraction is simply not being able to see the speaker. Often the seating arrangement at a meeting or in a lecture means people are out of view, or you see only the back of their heads. Not seeing often means not hearing – either because the voice is being carried in another direction or because we need to see a person to listen to them properly. Of course this has implications for how well we 'listen' on the phone, when all we have is a disembodied voice and no person whose body language can tell us as much as the words!

How we show we're not listening

Having discussed the many reasons we might have for not listening to someone, let us remind ourselves how we show we're not listening. Think, quite simply, of what you do when you're not interested and want to escape from the speaker or the subject being talked about. Do you:

● turn away

■ shuffle papers on your desk

▲ put papers away in a drawer

- have a glazed look in your eyes

- lack conviction or energy in your responses

- pick up a book and start reading

- turn and talk to someone else in the room

▲ continue to look at the TV (if you're at home!)

- not respond on purpose to a question?

These are just a few of the things we do when we're not listening. There are many others. But beware of judging the following behaviours as those of not listening:

- gazing out of the window: it might be a sign of concentration

- doodling: it might be a way of visualising an idea or of trying to understand a complex thought

▲ sitting back in a chair – it could denote comfort with what is happening.

So, although this guide is intended to help you become a better listener, remember that others also listen to you! Use insights you'll gain to become more aware, when you're speaking, of when you're not being listened to. And if this appears to be happening, the best way to find out is to ask the other person (or persons)! But rather than asking a direct question, which might come across as an accusation, a better way may be to remark that you think you've lost their attention or interest. If this is the case ask them what is stopping them from listening to you. Feedback of this sort can be constructive in the long-run, even if hurtful at the time.

3 developing your skills as a listener

Having read this far you are already well on the way to developing your listening skills. Why? Because being aware of the main factors which affect listening provides a firm base for improvement. So what more can you do? If some of the points in the preceding pages have struck a chord with you, the following suggestions may prove useful. Remember that they are no more than suggestions: undoubtedly you will be able to refine and add to them in the light of your own experience.

Helping yourself to listen

Perhaps the most effective way to improve your listening ability is to pay particular attention to your 'attending behaviours'. There are three main ways of attending: physically, psychologically, and verbally. It is in practice difficult to separate the three but we'll do so here, to emphasise each of them in turn.

Attending physically

Attending physically involves you, as the listener, adopting an attitude of involvement: showing the speaker that you are 'with' them just by your physical attitude or posture. The results of various research studies indicate that the following factors are important in physical attending:

- ● facing the speaker squarely
- ■ maintaining good eye contact
- ▲ maintaining an open posture
- ● remaining relatively relaxed.

Consider how you feel for instance if you are talking to somebody and they appear to be half-asleep. They may well be trying to listen but they don't actually look as if they are doing so. What effect does this have on you? The trick in attending physically is to let people see that you *are* listening. This is why the points outlined above are important. Each in a small way sends out the message to the speaker that they are receiving your undivided attention – and that it is worth their while to continue speaking.

For instance facing the speaker squarely shows that you are concentrating on what is being said. They see you listening because you are directly facing them and your attention isn't taken up by something beyond the window or on the wall. Your face is not being glimpsed past your left ear or across your right shoulder.

Good eye contact will also reinforce the 'I'm attending' message. Of course maintaining eye contact does not mean fixing the speaker with a wide-eyed unblinking stare: many people would find such a look totally disconcerting! But it probably does mean looking at the speaker's eyes rather more than you may do at present. Apart from anything else it helps to minimise the intrusion of visual distractions like the chart and calendar picture referred to earlier.

However, facing the speaker and maintaining eye contact are not enough on their own. To show you are really listening you should also adopt an open posture. Possibly the best illustration of these points is shown by your stance when you are listening to 'good' news, whatever it might be. You are 'all ears'; you don't want to miss a word! You aren't sitting with your arms folded, or too far away. Neither are you fiddling with your clothes, glancing at your watch, doodling on a piece of paper, making a close inspection of your finger nails, or doing anything else which might put the speaker off their stride. You are quite still, and are not just 'lending an ear' – you are offering both ears unconditionally. This is what happens when you really want to listen; and this readiness communicates itself very clearly to the speaker.

There is one final point associated with physical attending: being relatively relaxed. This does not mean being so much at ease that you look as if you are about to drop off! To be relatively relaxed involves showing the speaker a calm but interested exterior; this physical composure will quickly communicate itself to the speaker. But what if you're excited by what you're hearing? Is it wrong to show your enthusiasm? No. But if you get overenthused there is a good chance you will begin to listen to ideas going around in your own mind and stop listening so attentively to the speaker. It's a question of balance. On the other hand, if your speaker is upset; your calm posture will help them in turn to relax. Their behaviour will gradually begin to match yours. Such is the power of our behaviour on others!

But it is one thing to be aware of what is involved; it is another to put it into practice. Try in the first instance to concentrate, one at a time, on each of these points when you are listening to people. For instance, next week concentrate on the first point – facing the speaker squarely. In the following week concentrate on the second point – maintaining good eye contact. And so on. As you are concentrating on each point analyse your reactions in comparison with your former 'attending behaviour'. How much easier does it make listening to the speaker's message? It should have a marked effect on your listening ability and requires little effort to put into practice. Once you have developed your physical attending, the next thing is to concentrate on the message itself. This is known as attending psychologically. Be aware also of how those you are listening to are responding to your improved listening. Are they talking more? Are you hearing things you hadn't heard before?

Attending psychologically

Attending psychologically involves not only listening to what the speaker says but also attending to the non-verbal behaviour, ie to how it is said, and to the messages being sent by the speaker through facial expression, body posture, use of hands, and other physical indicators.

How do you learn to attend psychologically? To begin with you need to develop an ability – and willingness – to concentrate on the speaker and to:

- what is being said

- how it is being said

- what is not being said

- what feelings and emotions are being expressed, or not.

By focusing on the speaker and the subject being talked about, and clearing your mind of other issues, you become more aware of all the points just mentioned. You become aware of the speaker's voice and the speed at which they are talking.

Attending psychologically means not being drawn into or side tracked by any 'emotional' content of what is being said, but trying to remain a neutral listener, trying to see the speaker's point of view: stepping, as it were, into their shoes. To remain neutral is certainly not easy, particularly if the speaker is using emotion-laden words. However, if you can learn to interpret these words, and the body language that accompanies them, you will not only start to evaluate the message more correctly but you will also be giving yourself an opportunity to spot what is missing, what is left out.

Not interrupting – one of the main ways of improving your listening skills – is not easy, at least initially. You want to participate, to be drawn in and be part of what is being said. But you need to judge when the right time is for you to participate, and when it is the speaker's right to speak. To stop yourself interrupting, raising objections prematurely, and adopting a 'Yes but ...' approach may be difficult but its effect on your own listening, and what that produces, will be its own reward.

Attending verbally

Of course, to listen fully you need to hear, understand, and interpret what the speaker is saying. To concentrate on what is being said means listening for the central theme of what the speaker is saying rather than simply to individual facts, which are notoriously difficult to remember anyway. So, what is the speaker really saying? And if you don't understand the speaker's train of thought, or where there is something unclear to you, you need to question the speaker. This questioning in itself shows you are listening.

Do you know how *you* listen by:

- making eye contact?
- nodding or shaking your head?
- asking questions?
- summing up what the speaker has been saying?
- building on what has been said?
- avoiding other distractions: phones ringing, people interrupting?

However, these questions relate to what the speaker is actually saying. To listen with your mind also means listening for what is being said. It means assessing the meaning behind or between words. Part of this listening 'between the lines' concerns the speaker's purpose. You will find it difficult fully to assess the words without knowing what the speaker intends to achieve by using them. So, what might their intentions be? Are they trying to:

- gain personal acceptance
- justify a course of action
- sow seeds of doubt
- impose a viewpoint
- promote agreement
- release frustration
- explore self-doubt
- enhance a self-view
- 'butter-up'
- conceal emotions
- provide a waterproof shoulder
- seek support
- be deliberately provocative
- gain commitment

- clarify thoughts

- instil fear

- rationalise a situation

- make light of events?

In the same way that a critical evaluation of the words themselves is indicative of listening with the mind, so is an accurate identification of the speaker's intentions. These may not be quite so obvious as they first appear: the real purpose could be quite different. A speaker's ploys and strategies don't have to be recognisable in order to work! So both the words and the reasons behind them need to be questioned constantly. This questioning approach is a positive mental discipline which for most people only comes with practice: it doesn't just happen. It is one reason why listening really is active rather than merely passive, as some believe. It takes real mental effort to question continually not only what is being said but also why it is being said. As a consequence, listening really does involve rather more than just remaining silent!

To what extent do you take this approach when listening to people speak? Remember – to ask mental questions of this sort is one very real mark of psychological attention. To ask questions verbally is another. This factor is considered next.

Active ways of listening

Asking questions

Asking questions is a very positive way of showing the speaker that you really are listening. It not only gives them the chance to develop points further but also enables them to restate their case if you, the listener, haven't quite grasped the point being made. Listening questions will be ones that:

- show interest or encouragement, eg 'And then what happened?'

- seek further information, eg 'Can you give me an example?'

- explore feelings, eg 'How did you feel about that?'

- demonstrate understanding/clarify what has already been said, eg 'So it seems as though … '.

Summary questions are useful because they really show the speaker you've been fully with them, mentally and 'psychologically' throughout the encounter. Like reflective statements (see below) they will help you as the listener to interpret a speaker's words, but rather than reflecting emotional content the concern here is with factual content. Such questions can be used to review briefly, or to summarise, your understanding not only of the facts but also (and more importantly) the central ideas, the theme, of what the speaker is saying.

Questions like:

> 'As I understand it ... ?'
> 'If I've got it right ... ?'
> 'So what you're saying is ... ?'

are examples of this approach.

By using these various forms of question you show the speaker that you really are with them and want them to go on – to tell you more. They are another positive indication of psychological attention. Remember: skilful use of questions is another of the hallmarks of the truly effective listener!

All such questions need to be genuine ones, or ones you are asking as a way of supporting the speaker. They may also be challenging. But avoid being aggressive or confrontational. This raises the emotional temperature of the encounter, and once emotions are raised, listening flies out of the window! (For more on questions, see *Asking Questions* by the same author in this series.)

Giving encouragement

There are a number of ways in which you can encourage a speaker to say more, to expand on what they have already said.

Non-verbal noises

Non-verbal noises are a useful way of letting the speaker

know that you really are listening to what they are saying and, moreover, that you are sufficiently interested to hear more. Such noises are indications of attention, and together with appropriate facial expressions (smiles, raised eyebrows etc), head movements, and body posture, are a positive encouragement to the speaker to continue talking. The variety of encouraging noises that can be produced are extensive and the skilled listener, in varying the use of 'Hmm', 'Ah', 'Oh', 'Uhh' and other similar noises can encourage a speaker to continue indefinitely.

Supportive Statements
Supportive statements are the verbal equivalent of non-verbal noises.

Phrases like:

> 'I see … '
> 'And then … ?',
> 'That's interesting …'

are merely ways of saying, 'Go on, I'm with you – tell me more.' Used sensitively, such expressions will produce the same results as non-verbal noises – an encouragement to the speaker to go on.

Key word repetition
Key word repetition is a further way in which a speaker can be encouraged to say more. If you really are listening it will

not be difficult to pick out particular words or phrases which can then be used to encourage the speaker to explain in more detail.

Reflective statements

The reflective statement is extremely useful for exploring feelings in some depth. Again as the listener, you want the speaker to add to what they have said. But on this occasion, because you have been 'listening between the lines', you are 'tuning in' to the underlying emotions rather than to the factual content of the message. The most usual form of reflection is expressed as a statement and tends to begin with phrases like 'You feel that ... ?' and 'It seems to you that ...?'. These words indicate to the speaker that you are interpreting the emotional undertones of what is being said – that you are putting your finger on the deeper emotions behind the words and showing a real understanding of the speaker's feelings. In brief, you are displaying empathy – looking at the situation from the speaker's point of view. You are 'putting yourself in the speaker's shoes' – a skill which is positively identified with effective listening.

Question Form	Purpose
Non-verbal noises Supportive statements Key word repetition	To show interest/encouragement
Extension	To seek further information
Reflective statements	To explore feelings in detail
Summary	To demonstrate understanding/ clarify information already given

4 summary

In brief, then, what are the characteristics of the 'ideal listener' which can provide a target for you to aim at? In the words of one research study, the ideal listener:

primarily keeps an open, curious mind. He listens for new ideas everywhere, integrating what he hears with what he already knows. He is also self-perceptive and listens to others with his total being. Thus he becomes personally involved with what he hears ... He looks for ideas, organisation and arguments but always listens to the essence of things. Knowing that no two people listen the same, he stays mentally alert ... He is introspective but has the capacity and desire to critically examine, understand and attempt to transform some of his values, attitudes and relationships within himself and with others. He focuses his mind on the listening and listens to the speaker's ideas, but he also listens with feelings and intuition.*

And a few words in conclusion: many people think of listening as a passive occupation. The preceding pages have attempted to indicate just how active it really is. It is not a gentle pastime. It takes a very positive effort to become and

*From 'A definition of listening', unpublished master's degree thesis, Ohio State University, 1968, by Elizabeth Mae Pflaumer, summarised in S. Duker, *Listening: Readings Vol. II* (see Further Reading on page 61).

remain an effective listener. But the effort you will expend in so doing will be amply rewarded. You will be giving yourself every opportunity to develop as a person. Equally important, you will show you value and respect others – their views, knowledge, and experience.

5 exercises and activities

People develop skills by getting personally involved in their own learning. In other words they learn by doing, by personal experience. Experience may be a hard taskmaster, but there is a wealth of evidence that shows it is probably the most meaningful and durable method of learning. This is why people remember and apply the 'hot stove' principle: it is one thing to be told a stove is hot, it is another to experience it. You might touch a hot stove once, but twice? How long do you remember the experience before a painful reminder is necessary?

The activities on the following pages are a substitute for the hot stove! They provide a positive base for consolidating and developing listening skills.

If you do decide to incorporate any of these activities in a learning programme, remember that your task is to help people learn, *not* to teach them. The topic itself is undoubtedly important because of its effect on people's lives. How you help people to recognise this and develop themselves is even more important. As a sage from ancient times once expressed it, 'to listen well is a second inheritance' – he might as well have added 'so long as you use it wisely!'

Activity: *The listening week*

This activity is drawn from the guide that accompanies the video *Listen!* produced by Melrose and Ernst & Young – a highly useful resource when developing a programme on listening or communication skills training.

The activity may be used as the basis for establishing just how much time participants spend each week listening to people speak. It requires approximately 20–30 minutes to complete.

Begin by pointing out that far more time is devoted to listening than is generally appreciated. Follow up by asking participants to estimate how much time they spend listening to others during the average week. Remember (or perhaps note) the answers for later comparison at the conclusion of the activity. Then distribute the form shown on page 39 to participants for completion. A time limit for completion is probably not necessary.

Once everyone has finished, conduct a short analysis of the results. Post on a flip chart for great impact as shown in the example on page 40.

Activity: **The listening week**

Please estimate on the form below the amount of time you spend each week listening to people talk

My listening week

Estimated time
spent listening
each week
Hours/Minutes

At work:

In committee(s)

At other formal group meetings

At one-to-one formal meetings

In informal groups

In one-to-one informal conversation

On the telephone

Other (please specify)

. . . .

. . . .

. . . .

At home:

In any type of conversation

Leisure time outside home:

In any type of conversation

Other (please specify):

. . . .

. . . .

. . . .

TOTAL _____

Listening at work per week	
	No. of people
Up to 5 hours	. . . .
5–10 hours	. . . .
11–20 hours	. . . .
21–30 hours	. . . .
30+ hours	. . . .

Do the same for the remaining sections of the form and finally produce a composite picture of the listening week. Is it more or less than the *actual* working week of participants?

Finally, initiate a short discussion to consider the implications of the results, particularly in relation to the probable absence of previous formal training in listening for most, if not all, participants.

Activity: *Getting to know you*

This is another introductory activity. It provides a helpful background against which to explore some of the skills involved in listening effectively. It is also a particularly useful 'ice-breaker' for participants who don't know each other.

Phase 1

Participants are asked to split up into pairs. Each pair then decides who will be the questioner and who will be questioned (perhaps by tossing a coin – the person who calls correctly has the choice of either role).

The object of this phase of the activity is for the questioner to find out as much as he or she can about the other person. It is worth emphasising to participants that any questions regarded as unnecessarily intrusive need not be answered, or alternatively may be answered as seen fit.

Notes should *not* be taken.
Time: 5 minutes

Phase 2

The roles are then reversed. Again the object is for the questioner to find out as much as he or she can about the other person. The 'no notes' rule still applies.
Time: 5 minutes

Phase 3

All participants are then asked to report back, individually, what they have found out about their partners to the whole group. It should be emphasised that individuals may not require all the time allowed, but will be stopped if they overrun.
Time: maximum of 1 minute each

Phase 4

The group then re-forms into the same pairs and the partners discuss their reporting with each other. Questions which may be considered include:

- Just how accurate and full was the reporting? To what extent, if any, were assumed 'facts' reported to the group?

- How easy or difficult was it to remember what was said?

- Why was this?

- To what extent did mental 'rehearsal' for the Phase 3 feedback interfere with listening to others?

- On the basis of this experience what appear to be the most important pointers to improving personal listening performance?

Time: 10 minutes

Phase 5

The results of these discussions should now be considered in open session by the whole group. (A consolidated list of the agreed pointers to improving listening performance may also be developed and posted on a flip chart for future reference if this is thought advisable.)

Time: 25 minutes

It is suggested that the timings for the first three phases of the activity should be strictly adhered to. The timings for the last two phases are less critical and may be modified according to circumstances.

Activity: *Through the looking-glass*

In your introduction to this activity it is worth reminding participants that they spend far more time than they probably realise on listening to others.

Central to any exploration and development of personal listening skills is a genuine self-understanding. Explain that this activity is designed to help participants to get to know themselves better, to develop a closer self-understanding.

Phase 1
Distribute the questionnaire on pages 44–45 for completion by participants.
Time: approximately 10 minutes

Emphasise the following points:

● Participants should *not* spend a lot of time thinking about what they think they ought to write, but should put down whatever happens to come into their minds first.

■ The completed questionnaires will remain their own property.
Time: approximately 10 minutes.

Questionnaire

Don't spend too much time thinking about what you feel you ought to write. Write whatever happens to come first into your mind. Don't worry if you can't complete every sentence.

1. I'm quite happy to listen to somebody when

2. I tend to feel friendly towards speakers who

3. I don't like speakers who

4. When I look at myself critically as a listener

5. Irritating habits I find it hard to accept in a speaker include

6. Subjects I find it a little embarrassing to listen to include

7. I can get quite 'anti' when someone is talking about

8. As a listener, I get a bit nervous when

9. I get a lot of pleasure out of listening to someone talk about

10. A speaker gains my respect by

11. I tend to concentrate on what someone is saying if

12. If I can't put my 'two penn'orth' into a conversation I feel

13. I find it rather difficult to listen to someone who is talking about

14. As a listener I can get quite annoyed with myself when

15. Interrupting to ask questions when a person is speaking is

16. When I'm listening to someone speaking, I usually find myself spending most of the time

17. When someone is talking I think it is rude to

18. To become a better listener I feel I ought to

Phase 2
Individual participants should then discuss with a partner
what they have written.
Time: 10–15 minutes

Phase 3
The group re-forms to discuss the results.

Questions you may wish to consider include:

● What do the results show?

　 ○ Which particular questions produced notably
　　 different answers? Similar answers?

　 □ What are the possible causes?

■ Just how aware are people of what happens inside them
when listening to others? Like now?

▲ What conclusions can be drawn from this activity

　 ○ in general

　 □ for individual participants

　 △ for the organisation?
Time: 20 minutes

Activity: *The mirror*

'The face is the mirror of the soul' ... only the face?

This activity may be used as the basis for a discussion on the importance of accurately evaluating and interpreting non-verbal signs and voice-related signals.

In your introduction, emphasise that accurate interpretation of the speaker's non-verbal behaviour is a crucially important skill and that this skill cannot be developed overnight. Emphasise also that non-verbal behaviour cannot be evaluated in isolation but only in the context of the speaker's message and other related factors.

Many people are unaware of the effect their non-verbal behaviour may have on others. Research has shown that far greater credence is given to non-verbal messages than to what is actually said. Indeed, the following approximate figures give some indication of the relative importance attached by people to the component parts of a speaker's message:

Words   10%
Tone   35%
Non-verbal behaviour   55%

If a speaker's words are in conflict with his non-verbal behaviour it is the latter that will invariably be assessed as genuine.

However there is a considerable body of research on non-verbal behaviour so beware of oversimplification during discussion – remember that this activity is no more than an introduction to the subject.

Phase 1
Distribute the questionnaire shown on pages 49–50 to individual participants for completion.
Time: 10 minutes

Phase 2
Participants then form small groups of three or four to discuss their responses to the questionnaire.
Time: 15 minutes

Phase 3
These results should be discussed in plenary session by the whole group, conclusions should be drawn, and the implications of the activity for individual participants considered.

Conclusions that may result from this discussion include:

● Reliance on a single indicator will be misleading.

■ Some behaviours have *no* connection, eg an itch on the chin!

▲ Evaluation of a combination of indicators is likely to be more accurate but requires great caution.

◗ It takes considerable practice to interpret non-verbal signs accurately because so much depends on the context and what is being said.
Time: 20 minutes

As someone is talking to you, what do you think if he or she begins to behave as follows?

Opens his eyes wide

Blushes

Raises her eyebrows

Frowns

Smiles slightly

Purses his lips

Flutters her eyelashes

Tugs at his ear

Crinkles her eyes

Smiles broadly

Blinks rapidly

Avoids looking at you

Puts her chin in her hands

Leans forward

Nods intermittently

Looks at you steadily

Wags his finger at you

'Washes' her hands

Repeatedly folds and unfolds his arms

(continued on page 50)

Paces around while talking

Rubs her forefinger along her lips

Scratches his chin

Holds the bridge of her nose with thumb and forefinger

Fiddles with his tie or shirtcollar

Continually twines her hair round a finger

Puts both hands out towards you, palms turned up slightly

Steeples his fingers

Beats one clenched hand into the palm of the other

Scratches her head

Picks at his fingernails

Shrugs her shoulders

Activity: *Blackout*

This short activity is designed to give participants some experience of just how much a listener depends on non-verbal messages in order to understand fully what someone is saying. On a short programme it may be used as an alternative to the next activity, 'Recognising the signs'.

Phase 1
Ask participants to choose a partner from among the other group members. Then give the following instructions:

●   Sit facing your partner.

■ Close your eyes.

▲ Have a conversation on an agreed topic (for instance your personal objectives in being a member of this group).

● Keep your eyes closed for the entire conversation.

Tell participants that you will stop the conversation after 5 minutes.

Phase 2
The partners now discuss with each other how they felt during the conversation not being able to see any gestures or facial expressions, and consider which particular non-verbal cues were missed most.
Time: 5 minutes

Phase 3
Lead a general discussion to explore the results of the first two phases and to consider the implications for participants' personal development.
Time: 20 minutes

Activity: *Recognising the signs*
The purpose of this activity is to allow participants to practise recognising particular feelings in others by using non-verbal cues (eg tone of voice, inflection, speed of delivery) as they read out the text (see overleaf). Having explained this, ask participants to form small groups of four to six people.

Distribute the form and evaluation sheet on pages 53 and 55 to participants. Ask them to fill in the form as they hear each other speak.

Phase 1
Follow the instructions in the table 'Recognising the signs' on page 53.

Phase 2
The whole group re-forms to exchange views on what has happened so far. Questions which may be considered during this discussion include the following:

● Was identification of the feelings easy or difficult? Why?

■ Were particular feelings easier to identify than others? Why?

Phase 3
Individual participants now consider the results of this activity in terms of their own self-development as listeners, noting down the points they wish to follow up in the future.

You then summarise the main points of the activity, emphasising the necessity for individual commitment to development.

Recognising the signs: Form

1. **Please choose a feeling from the list below. Write down the feeling you have chosen in the box below. Do not tell your fellow participants which feeling you have chosen.**

List

Abhorrence	Depression	Modesty
Agitation	Despair	Nervousness
Amazement	Disappointment	Pleasure
Amusement	Disapproval	Prejudice
Annoyance	Dislike	Pride
Antagonism	Friendliness	Puzzlement
Anticipation	Fright	Regret
Antipathy	Frustration	Resentment
Apathy	Gladness	Reserve
Apprehension	Gratitude	Respect
Approval	Hope	Sarcasm
Astonishment	Hostility	Shame
Benevolence	Humiliation	Sorrow
Bitterness	Humility	Superiority
Boredom	Hurt	Tiredness
Caution	Importance	Thankfulness
Cheerfulness	Indifference	Tranquillity
Confidence	Inferiority	Virtuosity
Confusion	Joy	Vulnerability
Criticism	Jubilation	Wistfulness
Curiosity	Laziness	Wonderment
Dejection	Loathing	Worry

Choice

(continued on page 53)

2. Each person, in turn, now tries to communicate this feeling to others in the group whilst reading the following paragraphs.

Why is listening important?

Listening is the key to success. It enables you to do more than just hear what others are saying. Real listening means giving them your full attention, and understanding them. So, by listening you develop a deeper appreciation of what your colleagues at work are doing, how they are feeling and why; at home you understand more fully your family's hopes, fears and problems.

Listening opens up new horizons. It is the key to learning. In fact it is difficult to imagine how you could be successful without also being a good listener. As you become increasingly successful at listening you will recognise changes in yourself. Other people will recognise it also, and at least part of the pleasure of succeeding is that it is recognised by others.

But perhaps the greatest benefit of listening well to others is that they will reciprocate and listen to you, and respond to you when you are speaking. And the more you and they listen, the more you will all gain and learn.

3. Immediately after each person has finished speaking, the other group members complete the evaluation sheet. The figure on page 55 may be helpful for this.

4. The speaker now reveals which feeling he or she was trying to convey. Group members then share their assessments with each other and with the speaker. Conclude the discussion with an analysis of why consensus was absent, if indeed this was the case.

Recognising the signs: Evaluation sheet

Speaker	Identity of feeling?	Cues	Right/Wrong?

Sympathetic gestures

Proximity

Relaxed tone of voice

Smiles

'Crinkled' eyes

Expansive gestures

Warmth signified by

Aggressive posture

Harsh tone of voice

'Set' mouth

Distance

Staring eyes

Hostility signified by

Non-verbal communications

Speaking loudly/ quickly all the time

Ignoring responses

Interrupting

'Controlling' tone of voice

'Stabbing' fingers and other forceful gestures

Control/ domination signified by

Speaking quietly/ saying little

Allowing interruptions

Meek tone of voice

Downcast eyes

'Handwashing' and other nervous gestures

Submissiveness signified by

Activity: *How not to win friends*

Phase 1
Participants are asked to split up into groups of three or four to carry out the following task:

Discuss amongst yourselves the ways in which someone can show a speaker that he or she is really listening to what is said *even when not speaking or making any sound*. Draw up a list of these attending behaviours.

Phase 2
The full group comes together to discuss briefly the different types of attending behaviour identified. A consolidated list is agreed.

Phase 3
Individual participants join up into pairs. It is mutually agreed who will speak and who will listen. The speaker chooses a subject of mutual interest and talks for about five minutes on it. The partner should *not* follow any of the attending behaviours already identified in Phases 1 and 2. (In other words the listener should *not* face the speaker, *not* look at the speaker etc.)

At the end of five minutes (or probably sooner!) the speaker discusses with the partner the effects of this non-attending behaviour. Roles are then reversed and the same exercise is repeated.

Chartered Institute of Personnel and Development

Customer Satisfaction Survey

*We would be grateful if you could spend a few minutes answering these questions and return the postcard to CIPD. <u>Please use a black pen to answer</u>. **If you would like to receive a free CIPD pen, please include your name and address.*** IPD MEMBER Y/N

....

1. Title of book ....

2. Date of purchase: month .... year ....

3. How did you acquire this book?
☐ Bookshop ☐ Mail order ☐ Exhibition ☐ Gift ☐ Bought from Author

4. If ordered by mail, how long did it take to arrive:
☐ 1 week ☐ 2 weeks ☐ more than 2 weeks

5. Name of shop .... Town... Country ....

6. Please grade the following according to their influence on your purchasing decision with 1 as least influential: (please tick)

	1	2	3	4	5
Title					
Publisher					
Author					
Price					
Subject					
Cover					

7. On a scale of 1 to 5 (with 1 as poor & 5 as excellent) please give your impressions of the book in terms of: (please tick)

	1	2	3	4	5
Cover design					
Paper/print quality					
Good value for money					
General level of service					

8. Did you find the book:
Covers the subject in sufficient depth ☐ Yes ☐ No
Useful for your work ☐ Yes ☐ No

9. Are you using this book to help:
☐ In your work ☐ Personal study ☐ Both ☐ Other (please state)

Please complete if you are using this as part of a course

10. Name of academic institution..

11. Name of course you are following? ....

12. Did you find this book relevant to the syllabus? ☐ Yes ☐ No ☐ Don't know

Thank you!

To receive regular information about CIPD books and resources call 020 8263 3387.

1795/05/00

BUSINESS REPLY SERVICE
Licence No WD 1019

Publishing Department

Chartered Institute of Personnel and Development

CIPD House

Camp Road

Wimbledon

London

SW19 4BR

Phase 4
The full group reconvenes to discuss the implications of what happened for their own personal attending behaviour in the future.

Activity: *The oil can*

This activity is designed to help participants practise the art of 'lubricating' a conversation.

This oiling of the speaker's wheels may be achieved by using the sort of questions outlined on pages 30 and 31.

In your introduction emphasise that asking questions is a positive way of showing the speaker that you really are listening. The particular question forms which assist the lubrication process are shown opposite for easy reference.

Make sure you are familiar with the explanations of these question forms shown on page 33.

Phase 1
Ask participants to split up into groups of three and decide who will take the following roles: speaker, listener, observer. Emphasise that each person will gain experience of the other two roles as the activity proceeds.

The task is for the speaker to talk about one of the following topics:

Question Form	Purpose
Non-verbal noises Supportive statements Key word repetition }	To show interest/encouragement

1. My *best* experience in the last few years has been …

2. My *worst* experience in the last few years has been …

The task for the *listener* is to use the question forms indicated previously to 'lubricate' what the speaker is saying and as far as possible give encouragement. The listener should not use other question forms unless absolutely necessary. The task for the *observer* is to act as timekeeper and then lead a brief discussion on the listener's performance after the speaker has finished. The observer should sit slightly apart and remain silent during the dialogue.

Time for speaker: 5 minutes
Time for observer to lead discussion: 5 minutes

Phases 2 and 3
In each of these phases, the Phase 1 rules still apply but with a rotation of roles, so that all have a chance to experience the three roles.

Phase 4
Once everyone has experienced each role, lead a short discussion on the implications of this activity. Questions that

may be useful in this context are:

1. How easy or difficult was it to play the role of the listener?

2. Was Phase 3 more productive than Phase 1? Or less? Why?

3. What guidelines could be used in future to promote better listening?

Time: 20 minutes

further reading

ADLER A. *Communicating at Work*. London, McGraw-Hill, 1993

ARGYLE M. *Bodily Communication*. London, Methuen, 1988

BONE D. *A Practical Guide to Effective Listening*. London, Kogan Page, 1988

DECKER B. *How to Communicate Effectively*. London, Kogan Page, 1988

DUKER S. *Listening: Readings*. Vol. II. Scarecrow Press, 1971

ELLIN J. *Listening Helpfully: How to develop your counselling skills*. London, Souvenir Press, 1994

HONEY P. *and* MUMFORD A. *The Manual of Learning Styles*. Maidenhead, Peter Honey, 1982

IVEY A. *Managing Face-to-Face Communication*. Bromley, Chartwell Bratt, 1988

LEEDS D. *Smart Questions for Successful Managers*. London, Piatkus Books, 1987

LEWIS D. *The Secret Language of Success: How to read and use body-talk*. London, Corgi, 1990

MACKAY I. *Asking Questions*. 2nd edn. London, Institute of Personnel and Development, 1995

MURRAY H. *and* PAUL N. 'Training in body language'. *Training and Development*. Vol 8, No. 3, March 1990

NICHOLS R. G. *and* STEVENS L. A. *Are You Listening?* London, McGraw-Hill, 1957

ROBERTSON A. *Listen for Success.* New York, Irwin, 1994

THOULESS R. H. *Straight and Crooked Thinking*. London, Pan Books, 1981

WAINWRIGHT G. R. *Body Language*. London, Hodder and Stoughton, 1985

WAINWRIGHT G. R. *S.T.E.P.S. for Success: Self-training in essential personal skills*. London, Mercury Books, 1992

WICKS R. J. *Helping Others: Ways of listening, sharing and counselling*. London, Souvenir Press, 1994

Other titles in the *Management Shapers* series:

The Appraisal Discussion

Terry Gillen

Shows you how to make appraisal a productive and motivating experience for all levels of performer. It includes:

- assessing performance fairly and accurately

- using feedback to improve performance

- ▲ handling reluctant appraisees and avoiding bias

- agreeing future objectives

- identifying development needs.

1998 96 pages   0 85292 751 7

Constructive Feedback

Roland and Frances Bee

Practical advice on when to give feedback, how best to give it, and how to receive and use feedback yourself. It includes:

- using feedback in coaching, training, and team motivation

- distinguishing between criticism and feedback

- 10 tools of giving constructive feedback

- dealing with challenging situations and people.

1998 96 pages   0 85292 752 5

The Disciplinary Interview

Alan Fowler

This book will ensure that you adopt the correct procedures, conduct productive interviews and manage the outcome with confidence. It includes:

● understanding the legal implications

■ investigating the facts and presenting the management case

▲ probing the employee's case and diffusing conflict

● distinguishing between conduct and competence

● weighing up the alternatives to dismissal.

1998 96 pages   0 85292 753 3

Leadership Skills

John Adair

Leadership Skills will give you confidence, guidance and inspiration as you journey from being an effective manager to becoming a leader of excellence. Acknowledged as a world authority on leadership, Adair offers stimulating insights on:

- recognising and developing your leadership qualities

- acquiring the personal authority to give positive direction and the flexibility to embrace change

- acting on the key interacting needs – to achieve your task, build your team and develop its members

- transforming such core leadership functions such as planning, communicating and motivating into practical skills that you can master.

1998 96 pages   0 85292 764 9

Motivating People

Iain Maitland

Will help you maximise individual and team skills to achieve personal, departmental and, above all, organisational goals. It provides practical insights into:

- becoming a better leader and co-ordinating winning teams

- identifying, setting and communicating achievable targets

- empowering others through simple job improvement techniques

- encouraging self-development, defining training needs and providing helpful assessment

- ensuring that pay and workplace conditions make a positive contribution to satisfaction and commitment.

1998 96 pages   0 85292 766 5

Negotiating, Persuading and Influencing

Alan Fowler

Develop the skills you need to manage your staff effectively, bargain successfully with colleagues or deal tactfully with superiors. Sound advice on:

- probing and questioning techniques

- timing your tactics and using adjournments

- conceding and compromising to find common ground

- resisting manipulative ploys

- securing and implementing agreement.

1998 96 pages   ISBN 085292 755 X

Presentation Skills

Suzy Siddons

Presentation Skills helps you to prepare a well-targeted script with striking visuals and to fine-tune your performance so you can face an audience with total confidence. Invaluable advice is given on:

- researching your audience to understand their needs

- structuring your presentation to establish rapport, maintain interest and end with impact

- assembling ideas into a logical, persuasive sequence and transcribing key points onto overheads and prompt-cards

- rehearsing the delivery, projecting your voice and controlling nerves

- using question time to reinforce your message.

1999 80 pages   0 85292 810 6

The Selection Interview

Penny Hackett

The Selection Interview will ensure you choose better people – more efficiently. It provides step-by-step guidance on techniques and procedures from the initial decision to recruit through to the critical final choice. Helpful advice is included on:

- drawing up job descriptions, employee specifications and assessment plans

- setting up the interview

- using different interview strategies and styles

- improving your questioning and listening skills

- evaluating the evidence to reach the best decision.

1998 96 pages   0 85292 756 8

Telephone Skills

Patrick Forsyth

Telephone Skills sets out simple principles and techniques to enhance your communication skills and ensure you make a positive impact with every ring! It covers:

- taking calls – initial impressions, projecting the right personal and corporate image

- making calls – deciding what you want to achieve, establishing rapport and getting your message across

- using your voice, intonation and language to best effect

- listening attentively and knowing when to take the initiative

- diffusing anger and winning over difficult callers

- exceeding customer expectations and leaving a lasting impression.

2000 88 pages   0 85292 865 3

Transforming Your Workplace

Adryan Bell

With *Transforming Your Workplace* you can forget offices as grey, dull, predictable spots. Workplaces are becoming dynamic and exiting to reflect the challenge and pace of modern business. The benefits from simple workspace changes can be staggering, but equally it is easy to be fooled by fads and fashions. Adryan Bell, from an internationally renowned partnership of architects and ergonomists, provides expert guidance on making the difference:

- using new design solutions and innovative workspace models to enhance the way you work

- making simple changes – *feng shui*, fish tanks and fun

- incorporating the senses – style, colour, light, sound, smell, texture and comfort

- planning the projects to suit your needs and your budget

- wooing the die-hards and inspiring your project team.

2000 96 pages   0 85292 856 4